Steven C. Dunn, Ph.D.
Richard R. Young, Ph.D.

THE GREEN BARON
A BUSINESS ECOLUTION

Order this book online at www.trafford.com/06-2923
or email orders@trafford.com

Most Trafford titles are also available at major online book retailers.

Note for Librarians: A cataloguing record for this book is available from Library and Archives Canada at www.collectionscanada.ca/amicus/index-e.html

Printed in Victoria, BC, Canada.

ISBN: 978-1-4251-1164-9

We at Trafford believe that it is the responsibility of us all, as both individuals and corporations, to make choices that are environmentally and socially sound. You, in turn, are supporting this responsible conduct each time you purchase a Trafford book, or make use of our publishing services. To find out how you are helping, please visit www.trafford.com/responsiblepublishing.html

Our mission is to efficiently provide the world's finest, most comprehensive book publishing service, enabling every author to experience success. To find out how to publish your book, your way, and have it available worldwide, visit us online at www.trafford.com/10510

www.trafford.com

North America & international
toll-free: 1 888 232 4444 (USA & Canada)
phone: 250 383 6864 ♦ fax: 250 383 6804 ♦ email: info@trafford.com

The United Kingdom & Europe
phone: +44 (0)1865 722 113 ♦ local rate: 0845 230 9601
facsimile: +44 (0)1865 722 868 ♦ email: info.uk@trafford.com

10 9 8 7 6 5 4 3

FOREWORD

You are about to embark on a short journey with fictional characters whom, in fact, have become good friends of ours. The firm, Manor Industries, the city of Castleton and the nation of Hyperion are fictional. In essence, we have constructed a parable, a method of conveying lessons and important messages through storytelling. Recall, that parables were used frequently during ancient times, but are less common today, with the notable exceptions of Eliyahu Goldratt, author of *The Goal*; Ken Blanchard and his various collaborators of the *One Minute Manager* series; and Elliot Carlisle of the University of Massachusetts, author of *Mac*, and the person who introduced us to management parables. The reader may find that many of the conversations and positions taken by the characters may be fairly common–we have found similar instances among the hundreds of firms we have visited.

Note, too, that we are businessmen. Both of us have held responsible positions in several prominent manufacturing organizations, and even after career shifts to academia, we remain interested in business and the clear benefits that it provides to free societies. Moreover, we believe that as citizens of the Earth who need to live here, we must make every effort to assure that business systems and environmental systems are reconciled and function in harmony. Although this may sound like either heresy or an irreconcilable paradox to some people, we believe it is the direction of the future. Given the appropriate management culture and measurement criteria, sound environmental practice can be a significant source of competitive advantage that substantially improves shareholder value as well as preserving and nurturing the source of all of our lives and livelihoods: the Earth.

Each of the following chapters ends with a *So What?...*that will help you, the reader, gain this new perspective. Note, too, that by *So What?...*, we are using the popular idiom for *Why should I care about this?* or *Why is this important to me?* Collectively, these questions represent elements that must be considered by businesspeople seeking to change the way they think about the environment; they are the seeds of *Ecolution*.

We sincerely hope that you enjoy reading this parable as much as we have enjoyed writing it. Moreover, we hope that you will pass it on to your friends and colleagues, discuss or perhaps even argue over its message, and refer to it in the future. The *Ecolution* starts with you!

Steven C. Dunn, Ph.D.
Richard R. Young, Ph.D.

1

INTRODUCTION

THE DAY LONG MEETING WITH THE CORPORATE LEGAL STAFF OBVIOUSLY HAD TAKEN ITS TOLL. It was now 11:00 PM, and Baron was settling down in his study with a glass of mineral water just in time to catch the late news before heading off to bed. He was only half paying attention when the news clip showed a fire at a plant owned by one of his competitors. Sitting bolt upright, Baron watched as the news camera panned to show burning drums of toxic chemicals.

"Why can't these guys be more careful with that stuff!" Baron said out loud, even though no one else was in the room. "Every time there's an incident like this, we get the Feds crawling all over us, too, not to mention the protests going on outside our plants." It was a timely thought because the all-day meeting with the attorneys had dealt with how to respond to the ever-lengthening list of environmental and safety regulations that Baron's company had to comply with. As CEO, the burden ultimately fell on Baron's shoulders to affirm that everyone in the organization was on board, knew the company's environmental policies, and could transform those policies into responsible action.

"Damn! Why don't they know that responsible action is more than just expensive compliance–it's not just more costs to be borne, but a way to achieve competitive advantage," Baron said to himself, obviously deep in his own thoughts as the TV moved on to other news items.

"Yeah, Baron, you know now, but you didn't always. There was a time when you thought about the environment like the public believes most other businessmen think: take every advantage possible, perhaps even more when and if no one is looking." He remembered a series of events that took place eighteen months before–events that caused him to look at the situation in a totally different light.

It was then that he was shown that the proverbial glass was not half empty, but clearly half full. Baron's present fatigue and the passage of time had blurred his memory to many of the details, but he could remember that it was Warren, that bright young cost accountant, who played such an extraordinary role in transforming his thinking.

"But where did she get on to this? The university, perhaps?" Baron made a mental note to learn more about the process that had made such a dramatic change in his whole outlook on the issue. As he flipped the "off" button on his remote control, he made a further mental note to schedule a meeting with Warren for the following day.

Organizations react to events.
Environmental incidents are events.
Regulation is a reaction.
Therefore, there is a vested interest
in minimizing incidents.

So What?...Regulations are reactions
to environmental incidents!

2

THE PHONE CALL

"Good morning, Baron, I was surprised to get your call this morning. Is there something I can do to help you?" Warren asked.

"Well, in fact there is. You no doubt saw the news last night about that dreadful toxic materials fire at United Consolidated?"

"Sure," said Warren. "No matter what the cause was, it won't do our industry any good: it will be expensive for United Consolidated, but it also will be an additional cost for everyone else to comply with the new regulations that will result."

"That's why I called. Do you by any chance remember the series of events that led to our change of perspective? If we can identify those, we might be able to tell our story and convince others that being responsible can also provide exceptional competitive advantage."

Warren thought for a moment. "Gee, Baron, it just happened. I'll have to think about it a little because so many people affected my thinking."

"OK, take a couple of days. Is there a chance that you could stop by Friday morning and refresh my memory?"

Warren's response was no surprise, "Certainly, if it can help United Consolidated, it helps the whole industry. And that means Manor, too. Furthermore, if it helps the industry, it helps the environment, and I live here, too, just like everyone does, both here and at United Consolidated."

Organizations are groups of people. People require a quality environment. Therefore, organizations need to pursue environmental quality.

So What?...An organization's interest should not be different than the interest of the people who staff it.

3

THE MEETING

"WARREN, THANKS FOR COMING TO SEE ME. How'd your memory jog go?" Baron asked with anticipation.

"In fact, once I took the time to reflect," replied Warren, "it was really quite easy. You see, there were many people from both inside and outside of Manor who led me to think about environmental issues in a holistic way."

"Now you're jogging my memory, because I remember that the initial problem was the fragmented way we approached the issue: it was always an afterthought and nobody ever took ownership of it. Sure, we had an environmental manager, but the problem was that he approached the problem as an afterthought as well. We'd plan the business, and hope we were in compliance and that environmentally-related costs would be minimized. By looking at it in these terms, we were sub-optimizing like crazy."

"Exactly," Warren said.

"So tell me, who influenced your thinking?"

"As I said, it was many people, but like your comment on sub-optimization, each held only a very narrow or limited view of the problem," Warren replied. "All I did was combine all the issues, take a step or two backward, and build them into a business system, if you will. I know it sounds trite, but it was my mom and dad who first influenced me, perhaps in ways they themselves don't even realize."

"Your mom and dad?" Baron asked. "How did they enter into it? Although I do know that most successful women, and men, too, for that matter, have strong role models in their parents."

"That may be true, but it is not what I meant by their having an influence on my views of environmental issues in business.

Let me tell you two anecdotes, one with my mom, the other with my dad."

"Go ahead."

"About two years ago," she began, "while visiting my folks, I accompanied my mom to the grocery store. After picking up the items we needed for dinner, we went to the checkout line and the bagger asked us, 'paper or plastic?' Mom immediately said, 'paper, please' and said under her breath to me, 'you know, paper is far more recyclable than plastic. We've got to be environmentally friendly in this day and age. Besides, plastic doesn't decompose in landfills, certainly not the way paper does.' Remembering an article comparing the environmental impact of plastic and paper I'd seen in the *Wall Street Journal* and discussed in my MBA night class, I asked mom, 'What kinds of hazardous chemicals go into producing each, how much energy does it take to produce and transport, and what raw materials are required?'

"Poor mom knew that paper came from trees and plastics from oil, but otherwise she had no idea. So I told her that breaking down and bleaching wood fiber actually required a good deal of hazardous chemicals such as acids and bleach, that papermaking machinery consumes substantial energy, and paper does not decompose in landfills due to the lack of oxygen. She was quite surprised, which made me suspect that very few people really understand the complexity of this issue."

After listening to the story with his usual intensity, Baron said, "You had a pretty good grasp of what's going on, but chances are your mom uses only the popular press as a source of news. I wonder how many baggers in how many supermarkets ask that question on any given day, and how many shoppers give the wrong answer, or even the right answer for the wrong reasons?"

"Well, that's true," Warren continued. "But the second story was not long in coming. When mom and I returned home, we found dad up on a ladder fixing one of his birdhouses. Since his retirement, he has taken a keen interest in spotting the various species of birds that either live in or visit their region of the country. It turned out that dad had seen a variety of unusual thrushes for the past five years, but now there were none. When I asked him to tell me more, he said, 'At one time we had all sorts of birds here, but in recent years—now that I'm retired and can enjoy them more-they're gone. I don't understand it.' As a result, dad was not so much repairing his birdhouse, but enlarging its opening so that it could be used by some of the larger birds, robins and the like."

Baron interjected, "Hmmm, did your dad have any idea why he wasn't seeing as many varieties? Weather conditions or migratory patterns?"

"In fact he did. He suspected that the increased development in his and nearby communities was depriving many of these birds of their natural habitats. He had a unique way of looking at things and said that there may be no neutral areas, only positives and negatives: positive habitats attract and support species of wildlife and create no deleterious effects, while negative ones not only don't support wildlife, but require additional land to support the effects of that development. He used the term *sustainability*."

"So how did that affect your vision? You've given me two stories, but I don't see how it prompted you to look at a company such as Manor in such a different light."

"I don't mean to sound too theoretical, but it actually helped having been trained in accounting, where all accounts have debits and credits. When it's an asset account, we debit it to increase its value and we credit it to decrease its total value. When I look at the Earth as an enterprise, there are different types of asset accounts, some much more valuable than others, but there are also liability accounts–ones that we don't necessarily want to see get larger. I tend to think of it as the Earth's current ratio. Do you know the relationship of current assets to current liabilities?"

"You're starting to lose me now, Warren," Baron admitted. "Although I think I was with you up until about two minutes ago."

"OK," she said. "Say we think about natural resources as assets. When someone uses those assets, they can become liabilities. Liabilities, by the way, increase as a result of extractive processes, manufacturing, and consumption or use. Remember that my mom only looked at the disposal of her grocery bag and did not consider the liabilities created at other points in the supply chain, nor did she consider the use of resources, the debiting of the asset account, if you will."

"I think I'm starting to get it now," Baron said. "The more liabilities that companies like ours produce, the greater the cost borne by the entire system. When that cost becomes obvious, we get regulation, which in fact attempts to reassign that cost to us rather than to society as a whole."

"Precisely," Warren said. "And our ability to reuse or recycle materials ourselves reduces the amount that we credit to the Earth's liability accounts as well as reduce the amount of future debits that we will require from its asset accounts. The immediate effect is that we don't need to purchase as much material or require as much waste removal."

"Wait just a minute," Baron said. "That certainly doesn't come for free! Who's going to pay for that?"

"We already are paying for it, Baron. But it's not as bad as it sounds; it means that we are doing a better job of using the assets we do buy from the Earth's account. If the Earth doesn't need to pay, neither does Manor."

"This all sounds very nice, but there seems to be a major flaw," Baron countered. "Specifically, our competitors may not understand this crazy accounting system that you've concocted. I've got to admit that your ideas sound good over the long run, but what about those opportunists who only go for short-term gain?"

"There you go again," sighed Warren. "I maintain that if we take this approach, we are more competitive, not less. We make better use of the value contained within everything we buy, and we reduce the costs of getting rid of that which we don't want–a cost that I remind you continues to increase on a per unit basis each year. If we are careful, we can begin to call our liabilities, "unwanted assets," or items still containing value, and either reuse or sell them to others."

"Why do I think that we're back to that old 'is the glass half full or half empty question?" Baron mused. "I'm beginning to think that one person's waste is another's raw material. The problem is we've had the old thinking in place for so long that making any kind of change requires a Herculean effort. How do we accommodate that?"

"We can start by changing the way we talk about waste, like calling it a liability that can become an unwanted asset. One of the problems is that the Financial Accounting Standards Board does not provide for carrying most of this stuff on the books as assets. But we should really be thinking of waste as a raw material in the wrong place!"

"Part of the solution is to change the way people think. We've got to get them out of the narrow functional mindsets and into broadened views of both the environment and the business. But it's also where those two meet."

Baron considered this for a moment. "Getting back to that list of people you asked for," Warren continued. "It was my boss, Toller, the chief financial officer; Miller, the plant manager at Castleton; Chalmers, our environmental manager; Kaufer, the purchasing director; and Duffer, the director of international marketing, who really got me thinking. Each of them had a particular viewpoint that I recognized as being a part of the puzzle, even though many of them either would not or could not buy into the methods that I was using to relate the various elements to one another."

Baron thought about the people Warren named and realized that it certainly was a cast of different characters, but that clearly was also its strength. It was also apparent that either through direct control or indirect influence, decision-making concerning environmental issues had been highly fragmented, with little communication between individuals. Even worse, it sounded as if different measurement criteria might have actually forced each of these people to behave in conflicting ways.

"Interesting list, Warren," he observed. "But to get to the root of the decision-making process, the only thing left to do is to talk to each one, remind him or her of the conversations of eighteen months ago, and listen to whatever additional details each can provide. If you could find some time to talk to them, I think we might be able to piece this together into a strengthened program that we could use to convince others. What do you say?"

"Sure, I'll do it. It might even be fun to get reacquainted. I don't have much contact with them since I moved out of the division."

"Great," Baron said. "You never fail to leave me with even more to think about, but you have some people to talk to and I don't want you to be late. I will contact each of them and let them know that you will be calling. I'm looking forward to hearing whatever you might find out."

Systems are the coordinated functioning
of inter-related parts.
Businesses operate as systems.
The environment operates as a system.

So What?...Business systems are a
subpart of the environmental system.

4

MILLER–PLANT MANAGER

The United Consolidated news also was weighing heavily upon Miller, plant manager for Manor. It was 8:00 a.m., and he was standing outside the facility, observing the daily activity that makes up the life of a large manufacturing operation. As a switch engine moved a string of railcars containing inbound raw materials through the back gate, truckloads filled with Manor products bound for the final customers were leaving through the security gate. The morning shift was arriving, the workers parking their vehicles, and in these parts, that usually meant a four-wheel drive pickup or sport utility vehicle, in their appropriate parking spaces (even though spaces were not assigned formally, the informal organization structure of the workers nevertheless tended to allocate them). Miller turned to observe the plant buildings themselves, a mix of older brick and modern building composites. The plant had been in Castleton since 1912, and had seen its share of growth and change, both in the community and in the product line.

Just as Miller was about to go into the building, Parker, a young production line worker said, "Hey boss, did you see that incredible piece on United Consolidated? Could that ever happen here?"

Although Miller's immediate response to Parker was, "Not likely–we've taken every precaution possible and meet all of the government regulations concerning our hazardous materials," he knew that deep inside, a part of him didn't totally believe it. He began to wonder, "When did I became such a worrier about basic manufacturing?" He remembered the advice given by his predecessor, "Don't sweat all that regulatory B.S., Miller. Some day the government will come to its senses and realize that it's jobs at plants like ours that count and really do make this country what it is. They wouldn't dare do anything to jeopardize our facility's viability." That advice rang hollow at the moment with the UC disaster so vivid in his mind.

When Miller entered his office, he found a stack of paperwork and eight phone messages waiting, and his secretary informed him that Baron had phoned. "Great," Miller thought. "Just great! Another insane day on the old firing line."

Manor manufactures industrial products whose competitive advantage is based upon a process of firing components in an oven after they are given a proprietary chemical bath that contains an acid as well as several proprietary chemicals. The result is top quality products, but also a somewhat more dangerous workplace, with numerous residual chemical issues to deal with, including shipment, storage and on-site burial.

The Manor plant is located in downtown Castleton, next to the Fluess River. Until 1972, the waste from the plant was dumped directly from the plant into the river. In 1972, a citizens' environmental group rallied townspeople to demand a ban on dumping. Another citizens group, the mayor's "Blue Sky Air Coalition," currently was hounding Manor about its particulate emissions through the towering 70 ft. smokestack. When Miller was growing up in Castleton, the dark sooty air was a source of local pride, as it indicated jobs. The Castleton High School team was even called the Smokers. Now, some groups were calling for the company to leave town. "How times change," Miller thought to himself.

Manor's management had been slow to realize that the citizens groups indicated a significant change in the general public's attitude towards the environment, and consequently, Manor. The sight of protesters outside the plant was frequent during the '80s and early '90s. Ever since last summer when Warren, a staff auditor, asked about the capabilities of the firm to respond to a disaster, the CEO began to take the time and seemed genuinely concerned about environmental issues. Miller sat back at his desk, programmed his voice mail to take all his calls, and reflected on the consequences of that fateful meeting eighteen months ago.

He was deep in thought, when it occurred to him that he, too, had come 180 degrees on his environmental thinking. He used to believe strongly in the company and its ability to handle literally any situation, including environmental issues. He believed that the benefits Manor provided to Castleton–including jobs, taxes, support of local non-profits such as United Way, the local hospital and local school–far outweighed any little downsides such as the smoke released from the plant. Manor made Castleton what it was: Since the day it opened it had been the town's largest employer, and remained so today.

Miller grew up in Castleton. Both his father and grandfather had worked at the plant, and their earnings financed his college education. Miller was the first college graduate in his family. He returned to Castleton and started as a young engineer in the plant, gradually working his way to the top. Along the way, he married the daughter of a Manor foreman, and his wife was a seasonal fill-in in the packaging shop. They raised three sons and a daughter in Castleton, although none of them chose to stay in the area after they left school.

He remembered leaving the staff meeting that day more worried about the next shift's production than thinking about any environmental issue raised by a young junior accountant. Negotiations with the local union had occupied his thinking for weeks, when one day Warren, the same person who had asked the irritating questions some time ago, was waiting outside his office. He remembered saying something about being too busy to talk at that time, which in reality meant that he really didn't see any reason for them to talk at all. But, she had been persistent, mentioning something about an environmental audit of the Manor facility in Castleton.

He had invited her in, with the reminder that he had an important meeting with the union scheduled in less than a half hour. His office was that of a typical plant manager: lots of reports stacked on the desk, and photos on the wall of the corporate staff, his college degree, and subsequent professional certifications, but it was the picture of his grandson and him fishing that caught Warren's eye. The picture was taken a few years earlier on the Castleton reservoir. Miller had enjoyed fishing there as a kid, often hauling in six or more bass in a day. He remembered the tremendous pride when his sons caught their first bass–a feeling that arose again when he had the chance to take his first grandson out on his first fishing trip.

Warren had asked Miller if he still went fishing at the reservoir. Miller paused. Come to think of it, he hadn't been able to catch many bass in the last couple of years, between the limited season imposed by the Department of Fish and Game and the recent appearance of a species of carp-like sucker fish. Warren asked him if the dumping or smokestack releases by Manor had had any impact on the river and reservoir. Miller had often wondered what had caused the decline in the bass, but until she asked him that question he hadn't even considered the possibility that Manor had contributed to that decline. This was really a most disturbing thought.

The meeting lasted about a half an hour, covering mainly the manufacturing processes at the plant. Warren tried to understand his detailed explanations, but it was apparent that she had a tough time of it. He invited her back the following day for a walk through the plant so she could get a clearer understanding.

During the plant walk through, Miller realized he was not adequately addressing many of Warren's questions concerning their processes and procedures. It wasn't that he didn't understand the processes. Rather, he didn't really understand the whole picture and the relationships between daily operating decisions and the overall impact the plant had on the environment. For example, when they were passing workstation 17, where acid was added to the treating bath, she asked, "Where do we dump the residue from this process?" He realized that until 1972, they just flushed the system at the end of each shift and dumped the washout into the river. Since then, they still washed the system out at the end of each shift, but now they collected the washout, storing it in the same containers the acid came in, and when they had accumulated a truckload, transported it to a chemical processing facility 100 miles away. Storage, handling, transporting and final processing of the acid were currently costed as overhead items, proportionately allocated to each of the products, despite the fact that different products required differing amounts of acid to pre-clean each item. The EPA constantly watched the process. Manor had installed a monitoring station at its discharge point, and the firm not only had trained, but also had certified several workers in environmental response procedures.

Warren's next question caught him off guard: "Have we tried to substitute anything for the acid?" Miller couldn't recall any conversation in the past that prepared him other than the division R&D chemist saying, "Acid is the only compound that can effectively clean this particular product." He found himself repeating that comment by rote, but this time it seemed to ring hollow. He made a note to talk to that chemist one more time.

"Miller, that's a pretty weak response," Warren commented. "Surely we need to take a bigger picture look at the whole supply chain. Perhaps we could even bring in some of the suppliers, distributors and customers to discuss this whole issue?"

"Warren, I know there's been a lot written about integration of the supply chain, but unfortunately it's mostly talk of someone's crazy vision of what might be. Most firms don't have the slightest idea or capability to initiate any kind of coordination–they're just too busy with day-to-day operations. It really takes some strong individuals in each firm to recognize the opportunity and then have the initiative and ability to act on it. Information flow and trust in the network are critical, particularly when the various members in the chain have not always treated each other as partners."

"But what if we could treat each other as partners?" Warren replied. "Is there any way for you to initiate such a practice here in Castleton?"

"I haven't really given it enough thought," Miller admitted. "I'm sure I could start with a few key process components, particularly the acid. Let me think about it for a few weeks and see what I can do. This is exciting stuff: I wonder what our customers would say if we said we could produce the product without the hazardous materials? They're really the ones that have to deal with it when everything is said and done. I wonder what their disposal costs are. Do you think that our primary supplier would want to develop a substitute for the acid?"

"Could you prepare a report for Baron in three weeks?" Warren asked. "I'd like him to see that there are people like you inside Manor that can make these ideas operational. My fear is that Baron is going to hire a big consulting firm to come in and attempt to make this concept of environmental management happen. We'll be out big bucks, have a bunch of boilerplate notebooks, and then be left hanging with no concrete results. And that's more or less where we are right now!"

" I couldn't agree more," Miller said. "We have to do it ourselves."

Environmental management is more than
a simplistic disposal vs. recycling issue.
It starts with the design of products,
processes, and facilities.

So What?…The most effective way
to reduce waste is to not create it
in the first place.

5

CHALMERS–ENVIRONMENTAL MANAGER

CHALMERS, MANAGER OF ENVIRONMENT, HEALTH AND SAFETY (EHS) AT MANOR, WAS WORRIED. He had just received a call from Baron telling him that Warren would like to speak to him. He recalled that Warren was the accountant who asked the penetrating environmental questions at a staff meeting last year. He also remembered the interest that Baron had shown when he, Chalmers, couldn't adequately address her concerns.

They met the next day in his office, and Chalmers reminded himself not to be put on the defensive about any of the EHS responsibilities. People from other areas in the firm usually didn't have the foggiest idea what he went through on a daily basis just keeping Manor's back side out of the proverbial legal wringer.

"Good morning, Warren. How have you been? I haven't seen you since that meeting last year."

"I'm fine, Chalmers," she said, shaking his hand. "Yes, it has been a long time, and you definitely are one of the people I really wanted to spend some time with trying to better understand what you do."

Chalmers was flattered. "Most people look at us only as technicians that can wave some magic technology at the environmental problem and make it go away. Unfortunately, nothing could be further from the truth. This is definitely a management issue, and requires extensive analysis in terms of costs, benefits, and strategic positioning dependent upon our firm's values. Are you aware that nowhere in our firm's mission statement or strategic plan is there anything that says that the environment is an issue, let alone a priority in our thinking?"

"I have the distinct impression that that oversight will be changing in the future, given Baron's increasing interest in the environment," Warren observed.

"What makes you think he has an interest in the environment? I'm sure it's the usual temporary panic associated with a disaster, in this case the United Consolidated fiasco. People like Baron won't change. You know that he always will be interested in next quarter's stock price and his own bonus. He can't get too caught up in a nebulous area like environmental management. That's the only reason he keeps me around. I keep the government and the public at bay–sort of like a lion tamer. It's always potentially a deadly issue, but as long as you are professional and understand the issue, you can look it in the eye and make it do what you want."

"Is that your personal belief? That the firm should just keep the lion in check? Don't you have any worries about the environment?"

"I'm not paid to worry about it." Chalmers admitted. "I'm paid to keep it in control, but also not to spend too much of the firm's money doing it. Don't tell me you're one of these bleeding heart eco-centrists who believe that humans are only one part of the mix?"

"Who said anything about being a 'green'? I'm just interested in what makes you think you can control it? Don't you think that United Consolidated thought that they had control of their environment?"

"That's where you need to step up to the table, Warren. Technology in this area is constantly changing, and we spend most of our time trying to assess whether or not to make the changes required for upgrades. We're not naive here in EHS. We know that everyone in the firm only thinks of us as a costly but necessary operation. Our job is to make sure that those costs are minimized."

"And new technology is the answer?" Warren asked.

"Not always...at least not initially. But it certainly helps keep the public and the EPA off our backs. That's particularly true if it looks like we're doing everything we can with the latest equipment."

"Wouldn't they be more impressed if you made real, substantive long-term changes to the processes? I mean, really make an effort to change to a proactive methodology instead of end-of-pipe containment?"

"Again–and I must make this point strongly–the public and the government don't give a damn what we're doing in the long haul. They just don't want us dumping crap in the air and water. Consequently, whatever we can do to block that at any given moment gives us the biggest bang for the buck. I could no more get approval for a long-term change in process than you could make a change in the accounting practices of the firm. It's just not a realistic approach."

"So in other words you're telling me, 'Don't bother because this is the way we've always done it and always will?' So, who's the naive one around here?"

"Now don't go getting on your high horse, Warren." Chalmers said. "I only mean that realistically this ain't going to happen, so why spin my wheels in the mud when the only thing that will happen is that I get my overworked staff mired down in an exercise that won't result in anything being done and an initiative that will be gone as soon as the next one hits the firm?"

"Has anyone ever shown you the purchasing model where a dollar saved in purchase costs has the same impact as increasing income by a buck, or to put it another way, it might actually take $2-3 in sales to have the same impact?"

"Sure," Chalmers replied. "What's your point?"

"My point is that a proactive move earlier in the supply chain can have dramatic effects later on. In your case, if you'd work with plant management, purchasing, and our suppliers, you might be able to reduce your compliance issues significantly by making changes in the way we process or what we have to process."

"Warren, we can't just make these changes because of the environmental impact. What about our customers? They want the

Manor product, not some make-believe, greener image reincarnation of it. Besides, you're assuming that everyone in the chain is concerned about the environment. What a typical green thought. I don't think most of us are that concerned. Manor meets all federal and state regulatory guidelines: my staff makes sure of that."

"Why on earth would Manor want to spend money speculating on product and process changes that realistically may only have minimal effect on the environment?" Chalmers continued. "We are already meeting standards–standards set by some of the most knowledgeable scientists in the world. You've been watching too many *Nature Channel* diatribes that the sky is falling. Maybe you should see our new video, 'Manor and the Environment: Natural Partners.' In it, we explain fully how we monitor, contain, and treat all our hazardous wastes. In fact, there is even a segment that shows kids using that new nature park that we funded on the east side of town on that former waste storage site. Now if you'll excuse me, I have work to do."

"I'm very sorry that you feel this way, Chalmers," Warren said, picking up her coat. "I'm sure that we'll be talking again, and I hope that in the meantime you give some thought to the bigger picture. EHS does not just revolve around containment and should not be concerned with just meeting some arbitrary compliance measure at a given cost. There's a whole lot more opportunity here–opportunity to really change the way we operate and think about the environment, and I hope that you could help lead that change. I'll be in touch."

As Warren left, Chalmers leaned back in his chair and stared out the window looking at the Fluess River. Everything looked OK to him. Besides, what was she thinking? How could he possibly influence change in the firm? Didn't they pay him to control potential damage by monitoring for compliance? What did she mean, 'I'll be back'? How did she get so tight with Baron? I hope this isn't the beginning of another long crusade, he thought aloud. Just then, the phone rang. Probably just another crisis that has to be dealt with today, Chalmers thought to himself as he reached for the receiver.

The best technology needs to be applied
to environmental problems.
Technology must be managed by
increasingly higher levels of expertise.
High levels of expertise suggest issues
too complex for most people.
Removing people working
in other functions
from environmental concerns
is suboptimal. A systems approach
is optimal.

So What?...It may be a complicated issue,
but we need to keep everyone actively
involved to assure a successful outcome.

6

DUFFER–DIRECTOR OF INTERNATIONAL MARKETING

DUFFER THOUGHT THAT MANOR WAS A DREAM COME TRUE. After graduating from his MBA program, he advanced through the ranks at Manor, finally being promoted to Director of

International Marketing late last year. It was a great job, and allowed him the opportunity to travel worldwide in pursuit of markets and manufacturing opportunities for Manor. His work was mainly outside the office, conducted in remote overseas locations, researching favorable sourcing and potential manufacturing options for Manor. He reported directly to the CEO of the firm, Baron. Consequently, he was surprised to find a message from Warren, an assistant controller from another division, that she needed to meet with him as soon as possible.

Duffer had a hard time recalling exactly who she was. He vaguely remembered her making some comments about environmental issues a year or so ago in a staff meeting. Since he had not seen anything on the subject since then, he assumed that it wasn't an issue requiring further examination. He called her secretary and arranged to meet with her the next day.

Duffer had just returned from Hyperion, a country interested in having Manor build a facility in its second largest city, similar to the one in Castleton. The government of Hyperion had promised that environmental regulations–particularly those concerning sulfuric acid and smokestack releases–would not be an issue. Added to this was the fact that Hyperion had been suffering from high unemployment for several years, making the government's offer very tempting. Such a facility would be a boon to the country, providing jobs and renewed hope for many people.

The move to Hyperion also would be a tremendous opportunity for Manor to cut costs, particularly on the environmental side. If successful, it would result in closure of the Castleton facility, an old unionized operation with numerous environmental regulatory issues. Seeing no reason to continue being hassled by the U.S. government and local environmental groups, Duffer thought that if jobs are threatened, common sense would prevail and the firm could diversify internationally. At the moment, Duffer was also working on a deal with Hyperion for them to become a repository for the sulfuric acid containers and washout created from the production process. They were very interested since they had lots of unutilized space and could easily make the preparations to landfill or dump the material off their coastline.

When Warren arrived at Duffer's office, he decided that he could not afford to let her meddle in the already established plans. He wondered how she had managed to gain Baron's ear when she stunned him with a question concerning the status of the Hyperion negotiations.

"I'm anxious to hear about how the Hyperion project is progressing," queried Warren.

Duffer replied caustically, "Those are top secret negotiations involving only select members of our firm, and I am not at liberty to discuss them with you."

"I only asked because Baron mentioned the negotiations,

and I wondered if there were any environmental considerations that are not being accounted for that the firm should be aware of," she countered.

Duffer was surprised that Baron had confided in her and that the boss seemed suddenly to have developed environmental concerns. Duffer grew up believing that the environment was something to be utilized to one's benefit. He remembered being stunned when he learned how much money compliance was costing Manor each year, and how no one could ever seem to get away from the regulatory agencies in the U.S. This was why he was such a proponent of international sourcing. Countries like Hyperion, which had thousands of square miles of undeveloped land and potential resources, were more than willing to be reasonable with the by-products and residuals that manufacturing produced. They recognized that any manufacturing process affected the environment, not always for the best. However, economic growth was more important. Technology could be imported at a later date to deal with the environmental issues. The people's ability to work and increase their wealth was of paramount importance. America used to understand these values, but had gotten sidetracked by ne'er-do-well types that worried about things like snail darters, and the ability to put a price on pollution. If America wasn't careful, it would find that manufacturers would abandon her for 'greener' pastures.

Duffer's reply was carefully worded. After all, Warren had come at the behest of Baron himself. "Warren, I don't think that you have a realistic handle on environmental issues, at least in the context of other cultures. You have the luxury of being able to worry about the environment because you have always had a roof over your head, food to eat, and nobody trying to kill you. It's kind of like Maslow's hierarchy: how do you have the right to tell someone from Hyperion that the plant can't be built as planned because it might affect the air he breathes or the water he drinks? He couldn't care less. He has a family to feed today and needs the job just to provide the most basic human needs. Don't be so high and mighty. You might actually be affecting the welfare of children because you cause our firm not to make what is a financially sound decision for both us and Hyperion. Their government will worry about pollution if and when it becomes an issue; for that matter, so will we. Remember, it's all relative. What's considered bad here is not even an issue there."

"Duffer, I am very disappointed by your comments," she admitted. "I'm not here to attack you or to question your loyalty to the firm, but I really think that you are way out of line in terms of your understanding the significance of the environmental issues to Manor. Our actions, both operations and overall strategy, which includes global sourcing issues, directly impact the environment and the public's perception of our motives. This can result in negative publicity, plummeting investments in our firm, and an increase in government scrutiny, all of which may impact both our sales and margins, not to mention our stockholder equity."

"I hardly think the world worries about what Manor does on a daily basis unless they have a vested interest in the performance of the firm," Duffer said.

"Unfortunately, many firms have had to learn the hard way that what you are saying isn't true. Take Union Carbide, for example. The Bhophal disaster has certainly had long-term impacts on investors, employees, and the chemical industry as a whole, not to mention any chemical firm's relations in India. Today, Carbide no longer exists as a result."

"An unfortunate incident," Duffer said, "hardly likely that it could ever happen to us. But anyway, what's your real reason for being here today?"

Warren took a moment to collect her thoughts. The previous discussion had completely sidetracked her thinking process and showed just how far apart even the top management of Manor was in terms of a cohesive understanding of the environment, its importance, and its potential for the firm.

"Duffer, I'm here to discuss the interface of international operations and the environment. Can you honestly show me that moving operations to Hyperion won't have both quantitative and qualitative environmental cost implications that we need to consider in our decision making process?"

"How can we possibly estimate what might happen? I will calculate the usual estimates with sensitivity assumptions for planning purposes, but realistically it's a crapshoot. When we negotiate with countries like Hyperion, we have to deal in good faith with the leadership. They believe strongly that a personal relationship precedes and transcends business relationships. "

"My point exactly," replied Warren.

Duffer, realizing that he had walked into a jungle with the tiger, said, "Well, perhaps I should restate that last comment. Of course, we are aware that we would be moving our environmental issues elsewhere. But rest assured that we would handle them in the same, careful manner that we do here in the States. We just wouldn't have to deal with all of the reporting and monitoring nonsense that takes so much of our time and energy here. This is what truly adds to cost and gives us nothing."

"Are you saying that we would be doing things exactly as we do here?" asked Warren.

"Well, I don't know if they would be exactly the same, but they certainly would meet the requirements of the Hyperion government. It's not like we'd be dumping raw hazardous materials all over the place. Let me remind you, it's not the environmental costs that are driving the interest in this move, it's overall operational and logistics considerations."

We are all in this together.
The Earth is one system
Actions in one place will ultimately
affect the whole.

So What?...No part of the Earth
should be treated with less respect
than any other.

7

TOLLER–CHIEF FINANCIAL OFFICER

TOLLER WAS INTRIGUED WITH THE E-MAIL SHE JUST RECEIVED FROM BARON. He mentioned that the United Consolidated spill was weighing heavily on him. "He's not alone in that thought,"

she admitted to herself. Baron wanted Toller to meet with Warren to discuss the whole concept of environmental management at Manor. Toller had originally hired Warren, but Warren had moved out of the corporate office to one of Manor's divisions soon after a meeting last year in which she had questioned Manor's capabilities to respond to an environmental incident. How ironic that she should resurface so soon after the United Consolidated incident.

Toller had been with Manor for over 20 years and had moved up through the ranks to her present position because of her tenacious ability to sort through issues and make decisions that made common sense to all of the people around her. The fact that she was a female in a male-dominated industry had not impeded her, at least not that she was aware of. This was largely because she was so effective at getting the job done right. She was wondering why Warren was Baron's point person on this project when her assistant buzzed her that Warren was on the line.

"Warren, how are you doing? It's been a long time."

"I'm doing very well, Toller, thanks to the wonderful training I got from you."

"I'm flattered, but I think you're doing quite well on your own. What can I do for you?"

"Baron asked me to meet with a number of people in the firm to get an assessment of where we really are in terms of environmental management. As you are most certainly aware, United Consolidated has really been in the news these past few days, and I'm sure that sparked Baron's concern, especially since we sell to many of the same markets and use similar raw materials. I don't think any of us didn't cringe the other night when we heard the news. I can't think of anything worse for a firm than that kind of negative publicity, particularly when you try to deny responsibility for the events leading to the spill. Their accident even caused our own stock price to drop a few points."

"I couldn't agree more," Toller said. "I'd like to talk with you about Manor's history and financial exposure to such events in the context of what we can do to position ourselves differently should the necessity arise. Would tomorrow at nine be OK?"

"Tomorrow at nine it is. See you then."

Toller hung up the phone and thought about how she would handle Warren tomorrow. She had to be careful, since Baron was obviously overseeing this little endeavor. How could she explain that the environment was not exactly a top priority with the financial group, other than as a potential liability issue? Personally, she almost couldn't care less.

Toller moved to Castleton from New York City when she took the Manor Industries job, and to this day viewed the place as a paradise compared to her hometown and the other cities she traveled to. What was a little smoke, compared to the intense smog and traffic of the city? Besides, as a newly appointed (the first female) deacon in her church, she strongly believed that humans were destined to rule the earth, and that God had given them a mandate to use the resources as necessary. She decided to put together a little presentation that would show Warren and Baron the exact cost of environmental containment to Manor.

The next morning, Warren began the meeting showing Toller a short video of a special news documentary on the risks posed to ordinary citizens by companies that dealt with hazardous materials. It played on one of the major networks last night just prior to the news, where the president of United Consolidated was being interviewed. He admitted that the firm had cut corners in terms of their environmental reporting and procedures, and vowed that it would not happen again. Even to an experienced insider like Warren, he appeared to be hedging, trying to carefully pick his words. He did not seem quite trustworthy. The early morning stock report showed that the public agreed with her assessment. Manor stock had dropped another four points–guilty by association.

"Warren, as CFO, one of my primary responsibilities is the financial health of this company," Toller began. "I am acutely aware these incidents have a direct impact if not handled promptly and thoroughly. That is why we have just issued a press release that details Manor's history of environmental compliance and awareness.

Chalmers will be on the network's noon talk show today with his video. Hopefully, that will stop the hemorrhaging and show people that some of us really do handle hazardous materials with care. If we can weather another few days, this tempest will blow over and we can go back to focusing on what we do best: producing high quality products, delivered on-time at competitive prices, and providing a stable job base for the people of Castleton. So what did you have in mind this morning?"

"Business as usual?" Warren wondered. "I hope you're joking. This United Consolidated incident is exactly the type of incident that we must avoid at any cost."

"Don't get carried away with this green concern, Warren. We still have to be profitable for any of us to have a job. Let me explain how we calculate environmental costs here at Manor. First, all of the direct costs of compliance are accumulated by Chalmers' EHS group. We typically budget a certain percentage of our gross revenue for this. His costs have risen consistently at about 5% per year for the past five years, mainly due to the increase in legal activity. Once the direct costs are calculated, they are allocated to the various products that incur them. Indirect costs such as inspections are allocated evenly across the board. We try to keep his staff level constant, particularly since we anticipate a reduction in regulations based upon conversations with our senator. By the way, since when did you get so carried away on this environmental crusade?"

Warren smiled, "I know that I must sound like a zealot, but this is about our future and it is precisely about our jobs. It involves long-term investment strategy and capital expenditures that don't necessarily have that one year payback that we cherish so much. It also involves our stock price, and why people might be interested in buying our stock above and beyond short-term performance. Is this more realistic?"

"Don't give me this airy-fairy stuff. This company isn't about to absorb a bunch of expenses just because it makes us feel good. We aren't about to abandon our successful financial formula for a social fad scheme that might be over next year. I hardly think anyone in this town is going to be screaming for environmental investments when we explain that because we aren't cost competitive, most of the operations will be moving to Hyperion."

"What have you been doing in terms of the Hyperion operation?" Warren asked.

"That is still highly secret and hardly any of your concern," Toller replied curtly.

"I had a very in-depth discussion of the issue with Duffer just the other day, Warren replied. "I hope you are looking at potential direct and indirect environmental costs in your model."

"Again, I hardly think that you need concern yourself with what we are considering in our calculations. Is this all we had to talk about today?"

"Are you at all concerned about the ethics of your positions?"

"What? Of course we strive to maintain the highest moral ground on all of our actions. As a CPA, you should understand the importance of ethical behavior in finance."

"That's not what I'm getting at," Warren said. "What about the investment calculations? Do they include anything for the qualitative aspects of the environment that they impact–the commons so to speak?"

"How on Earth do we quantify the value of clean air?" Toller asked. "Of clean water? A nicer town to live in? Is this our responsibility? People value us on the basis of what we do. We provide jobs and invest in the cities and countries in which we are located. We use the latest technology in our environmental compliance, follow all of the FASB standards for accounting, and meet any compliance regulation the government requires. Would our shareholders want us spending money on anything other than what we are required to do or that which adds value? How does being an environmental good guy add value, when you can't even get scientists, the government, citizens or environmentalists to agree on what's good or bad for the world?"

"When was the last time you spent time really assessing our costs with Miller?" Warren asked Toller. "I think he has some ideas that might just change that opinion. He really believes that changing a few of our processes might, in fact, add value both to the environment and to our firm."

"Miller would sell his soul if he could make his plant more efficient. He knows we're looking at sourcing production to Hyperion."

"Precisely," Warren said. "Don't you see that it finally takes a major catastrophe to get people moving? Because of the potential closure, Miller has finally recognized that certain actions may make this facility far more cost effective in the long run. How can you say with certainty that the people of Hyperion won't balk if we put in a plant that utilizes hazardous materials that will then have to be handled by their country? How can you ethically support a move that would take advantage of another society's economic desperation in exchange for a cheaper way of doing business, but one that is neither materially nor morally right?"

"I resent your implications that my ethical imperatives are anything but pure," Toller said. "I remind you that I am a deacon in my church and am a CPA. I am recognized for my high ethical standards, both personally and professionally. Moving a production facility has nothing to do with ethics. What about the desires and needs of Hyperion?"

Toller was definitely flustered by the implication. She thought to herself, "How could anyone not think that I have the most honorable intentions in business and personally? That I am not acting in best interests of the employees and the shareholders?"

Warren shrugged her shoulders and rose to leave. "I hope you'll give some more thought to the topics we discussed today and that you'll understand that I didn't come here to question your motives or ethics. I simply would like to see us take a different perspective in how we look at the environmental equation, particularly in terms of financing issues. Perhaps, after we have both cooled off, we could get together and reassess the situation?"

Toller decided to wait and see if Baron responded to her directly. It would not make any sense for her to do anything until she was certain that he wanted her to spend time on this subject.

"Warren, I'm sorry I got so heated, but my schedule is quite full for the next few weeks and…I'll be in touch."

Warren left the office depressed. How could she have blown this opportunity to impress upon her former mentor the importance of this new perspective, and how it would be a permanent part of any firm's financial equation from now on? She decided to take a long drive before returning home to prepare her thoughts prior to reporting back to Baron.

Classical economics considered
only land, labor and capital.
Environmental issues were externalities.
Accounting has traditionally
ignored externalities.

So What?...Our economic theories and
accounting systems will need to change
to embrace environmental concerns.

8

LESSONS ALL AROUND

About a half hour out of town, Warren noticed the fuel level warning light flashing on her dashboard, so she decided to stop at the next available station to fill up. She saw a rather new Subterra Oil Company station up ahead and pulled in. Immediately, she was surrounded by three attendants, one asking her if she needed a fill up, the other already cleaning her windshield, and the third checking the air in her tires. She was amazed. Weren't they also advertising the lowest gas prices in the area? How did they do it? How did they get employees to hustle, and provide services that other dealers had long since abandoned? Weren't Subterra Oil stations sprouting up all over the area? She asked the attendant who had initially taken her order and who was now checking her oil, why he worked so hard.

"It's the way we operate, ma'am."

(Warren was not used to being addressed as ma'am, and it made her feel suddenly a little out of touch.) "The way our station manager explained it to me is that the most important thing for us to do is please the customer by providing prompt, courteous service," he explained. "As we gain more customers and sell more product, we are able to keep our prices low. Sure, we don't have to be a full service station. Hell, almost nobody else is any more, but this is what our customers have come to expect, and they will drive right past a competitor's station even if his gas price is 5¢ a gallon cheaper. We've found that price isn't everything. At the same time, we figured out that we can create an image that our customers identify with, and in return want to do business with us."

"Makes sense," she said smiling. "Thanks."

“Thank you for coming to Subterra,” he said, giving her windshield one last touch of his towel.

Warren made a mental note to call the station manager to get more details, but her thoughts were already far away, her mind racing with the parallels between the added service and the day’s earlier discussions concerning Manor’s operations, particularly the similarities between quality of service and their application to environmental processes in her firm. Myopic cost containment might lead to profits in the very short term, but almost always has proved unsuccessful over the long pull.

Competitive advantage is achieved
by increasing marketplace value.
Value can be defined as the ratio
of functionality to cost.
Improved environmental practices
can increase functionality.

So What?...Sound environmental
practices will be a source of competitive
advantage and goodwill.

9

KAUFER–PURCHASING DIRECTOR

WARREN ARRIVED AT THE PURCHASING DEPARTMENT, HER FIRST STOP ON THE DAY'S ITINERARY SET UP FOR HER BY BARON. She found it much easier getting in to see people when the CEO made her appointments. What a contrast with her experience two years ago when, as a junior staff cost accountant fresh out of the state university, she was viewed as either a pain in the neck, a threat because that's how anyone from accounting was viewed, or a 'greenhorn' who didn't understand the business and had no place taking up the time of anyone who was keeping things going on a day-to-day basis.

"Warren," Kaufer greeted her pleasantly, "nice to see you again. How's the new job treating you?"

"Things are just fine, Kaufer. Thanks for asking," replied Warren. "I assume Baron explained to you the reason for my visit?"

"Yeah, he did. He said something about trying to figure out what made us change the way the company considers the environment within the framework of its whole business."

"Right. Baron saw that United Consolidated disaster on TV the other night and wants to be sure not only that such a thing can't happen here, but also that our strategic vision–particularly the way it's carried out–is a program that can be applied elsewhere. Hopefully, we can find a way to preclude others from making more environmental blunders, while making our suppliers more competitive and lowering their costs, which in turn would lower what they charge us."

"Right," Kaufer replied. "I remember some of the discussion

we had last year. You came around to ask questions about the amount of money we earn from metals salvage, how much we spent on dumpster removal, and our options in terms of recycling and reuse instead of hauling. You made quite an impression on my staff. We managed to get a few more bucks back from plastics recycling and avoided some purchase expenses by not filling up the dumpsters so often."

Warren smiled. "I also seem to remember some talk about related disposal issues, particularly how purchasing costs could be reduced by relating the items being purchased to their ultimate contribution to the residuals stream. This would enable us to avoid many disposal costs and reduce purchase costs."

"That worked well when we first tried it," Kaufer observed. "We really saved the firm some bucks in the first pass. But it took a lot of my buyers' time, particularly out on the production floor with the operating types. So we discontinued it last year. Besides, we're a 'close to the action, hard hitting type of shop' here. Our reputation ebbs and flows on how well we can place orders. We still measure buyers by how many orders they can place, how many dollars they can save, and how many late deliveries we can avoid. It's simple: if you're one of my buyers, you have to stay chained to your desk with an ear on the phone. Roaming around on the production floor doesn't win us any points around here. Certainly not with me. Now, I know Baron sent you to see me, and I don't mean any disrespect towards you or him, but environmental issues don't pay the bills, if you know what I mean. Besides, we thought this was another plan *du jour.* You know, like total quality management, just-in-time delivery, and process re-engineering. They all come; they all go."

"Interesting observations, Kaufer," Warren said. "That means that you haven't changed the way you do business, but only gave us 'flash in the pan' results back eighteen months ago. Hasn't anyone noticed? No more meetings?"

"I don't mean to rain on your parade, Warren, but that's about the size of it. You're smart, so why don't you get off this kick and try something in mainstream business instead of an afterthought like industrial waste?"

It's been said elsewhere:
*"Only those things that get measured
can be managed."*
But also,
*Constantly emerging management fads
create many skeptics.
Skeptics are usually resistant to change.*

So What?...Environmental concerns
should not be
just another management fad.
They are a strategic survival imperative.

10

CHANGES OR NO CHANGES?

Some days later...

Scribner, Baron's secretary, looked up as Warren approached. "I hope you've got good news for him," Scribner said. "The only thing he's been thinking about all morning is the briefing that you're to give. Go on in."

"Thanks, Scribner. Keep your fingers crossed for me," Warren said opening the door.

"Warren, have a seat," Baron said. "I can't wait to hear the results of your discussions. Everyone cooperatived with you, I hope. Now tell me everything–both the good and the bad–what you've learned."

"Well, I have started to sense that my role has shifted," Warren began. "While our mutual intentions were for me to be able to recall how the company shifted its thinking, I now must tell you that I feel my role has become akin to an internal consultant. I find that much of the company's thinking has, in fact, not shifted. Let me repeat, our thinking has NOT shifted."

Baron could not contain his emotions. He rose up out of his chair and bellowed, "What do you mean by 'NOT shifted'? I thought we had buy-in nearly two years ago. What the hell happened? More important, how do we fix it? We're talking about what I believed was our competitive advantage–an advantage that you're now telling me we didn't lose to any competitive action, but internally chose to freely abandon?"

"That's about the size of it," Warren admitted. "Let's start with production. Clearly, Miller understands the two roles he plays–the first as production manager, the second as private citizen–and that these do affect each other on a continuing basis. Miller is worried about not being able to take his grandson fishing, so he sees that there is more to environmental concerns than controlling the disposal of waste. He continues to pursue materials substitution initiatives that will use more friendly materials, either because they have less hazardous properties or because they would provide better yield factors and produce less waste overall. New processing equipment has these two requirements built into their criteria for identifying potential suppliers, so these benefits will continue to increase. In addition, Miller is now looking to adopt some activity-based costing techniques that will allow him to charge those parts of our operation that produce the biggest disposal problems with their fair share of the cost. The cross-subsidization of the past will disappear, as nobody will be able to ignore who's doing what. Better yet, improvements can be readily seen rather than dumped into a catch-all overhead account. He has also recently investigated installing more energy efficient lighting in the plant and warehousing areas. But, so much for the good news."

Baron shook his head. "You mean that's it?" he asked, obviously still upset by what she'd said at the outset of their conversation. "Well, at least production influences a lot of other activities within the firm. Better let me have the bad news."

"Last year we thought purchasing had bought into the program. They got their buyers involved, had them spend lots of time in production, found new sources, challenged suppliers to use less packaging or substitute friendlier materials, and reduced the cost of waste removal. They even began to consider the environmental records of each supplier and those that couldn't pass muster were put on notice, although now that I think about it, I never heard of suppliers being dumped because of this. Unfortunately, purchasing's initiative didn't last. Kaufer has a short-term, transaction-based focus and believes that his greatest contribution to Manor is through buying materials at lower prices. Moreover, Kaufer's opinion on this initiative–and this was stated to me with all candor–is that, quote, 'the environmental focus is just another management fad that was gleaned from either a locker room conversation at someone's country club or from one of the titles carried at an airport bookshop.' If we goofed, it's because we couldn't convey the message that this issue is here to stay, that end-of-pipe solutions do not work, and that environmental considerations need to be woven into the very fabric of our firm. Fortunately for all of us, Kaufer's operation is driven substantially by Miller's requirements."

"But we also have an environmental manager whose job is to keep us out of hot water," Baron said defensively. "What's Chalmers doing for us?"

"Chalmers seems to do an OK job of keeping us in compliance with those requirements of the moment, but he's pretty much an 'end-of-pipe' thinker who's willing to seek out the technology necessary to treat whatever effluents we create. He claims that efforts to reduce volumes, substitute materials, and modify production processes and work to make our suppliers aware of our environmental needs is beyond the scope of his responsibility. However, he does get involved in performing the necessary due diligence on the annual bidders to the dumpster hauling and hazardous materials removal contracts. Because he's a trained engineer, Chalmers is very knowledgeable about emerging treatment technologies, and is convinced that therein lay our only responsibilities."

Baron massaged his temple. "Warren, you're depressing me. What's it going to take to make this damn thing happen? A revision to our corporate mission statement? A dedicated page in our annual report?"

"Well," she began, obviously flustered.

Baron interrupted her. "None of this is your fault, and I shouldn't be shooting the messenger."

Warren smiled. "I'm afraid that I began to tread into a sensitive area when I went to see Duffer about international initiatives. Until he told me, I didn't know that the Hyperion project was off limits for me to discuss. While I agree that the U.S. regulatory climate is costly and frequently forces companies like ours to make the wrong decisions, such as moving offshore, those cost advantages should not encourage us to abandon our principles for short-term gain, even if one could be had. We have made environmental responsibility a source of our competitive advantage, an advantage that goes with the company no matter where it goes. More than anything, I guess I'm most disappointed with the business as usual stance Duffer and some of the others are taking. It's like looking at our competitors and assuming that they know what they're doing and we don't, therefore we should emulate them. While I wish the situation were better, it isn't and the first step to fixing it is to realize that."

"It's tough to be first, or at least one of the first," Baron told her. "I can't believe that we're the only organization that's attempted to use the environmental issue as an integrated part of the business. But I guess it's no different than being a kid, when going along with the crowd offers a certain amount of acceptance by one's peers. Some folks say 'Why not?–not that many people could be wrong.' But these people can still be uninformed or misinformed. Our task, Warren, must be to find a way to change that, and we should probably begin with measurement criteria, which, by the way, makes me wonder about your meeting with Toller."

"Surprisingly, she was not any different than most of the others," Warren told him candidly. "I was disappointed by this. After all, she hired me into the firm and was my first mentor. Toller can relate environmental concerns to the price of our stock, but she is not willing to see the competitive advantage aspects that you and I have talked about. I guess as accountants, we have opposing philosophies.

"I feel that cost or managerial accounting needs to support the ability to make informed decisions. On the other hand, Toller sees it as completely subordinate to financial accounting, with the latter dictated by the standards of the FASB. It's not that Toller is either for or against environmental considerations; it's just that they're not part of her paradigm. You might say that it's a problem of being ahead of the curve, and as an accountant myself, I can tell you that our training doesn't normally encourage, let alone produce, risk takers. Baron, I've probably failed at the mission you asked me to do. I'm sorry."

"On the contrary," Baron said. "You've performed a very valuable service. I needed to know that we lost the advantage that I thought we had. And perhaps–and this is a very large 'perhaps'–you are the catalyst to bring us back to reality. I've decided to bring the group back together and let them build the criteria for getting us back on track. As CEO, I could dictate what should happen, but how much buy in would I achieve by doing that? Probably not much more than I have right now. Would you be willing to attend? If so, I'll have Scribner set it up."

"I'd really like to be there," Warren replied. "Although I should probably tell you that some of the people I spoke with think that both this issue and I are pains in the neck. I suspect

I'll have only marginal value at such a meeting. What I would like, though, is a phone call telling me how it went."

"As usual, you're probably right. OK, I'll let you know, but thanks again for everything."

That which is not constantly reinforced, regresses.

So What?...Environmental concerns require continuous reinforcement and ***ecolutionary*** thinking.

11

FIGURING THINGS OUT

THE PHONE RANG. "Warren, it's Baron."

"Hello, Baron. How'd your meeting go?"

"That's the reason I'm calling. In fact it went very well, although the discussion took some odd twists."

"Tell me more. Did you manage to get everyone on-board?"

"I did," he said. "But the person who really made the difference at the meeting was Miller. Your meeting with him made the first real convert. That modified cost accounting procedure you gave him allowed Miller to better understand what he was producing in terms of residuals, which allowed him to attack the most expensive sources. Mind you, these are only on paper at this point because he needs time to implement, but he clearly made impressions on Kaufer, Toller, and Chalmers. Since Miller is Kaufer's most significant internal customer, production's orientation almost by default becomes purchasing's. Scheduling meetings with key suppliers is already in the works."

"Great," Warren said. "But how were the others won over?"

"Well, I had hoped that there was some common sense in the decisions. There might have been, but I suspect there was also a healthy dose of self-interest. Toller started to look at the drop in cost of goods sold that Miller was forecasting. She was a hard sell at first, but eventually she conceded that the yield results had to speak for themselves. You accountants can be a strange lot."

Warren couldn't help smiling at the comment.

Baron continued, "Finally, Chalmers saw that as waste levels would decrease, he would need to take on a different role if he wanted to be seen making a contribution other than being our in-house daily reader of the *Federal Register.* He's begun to recast himself into an internal consultant and is smart enough to see Miller as his major customer."

"What about Duffer?" Warren asked. "He seemed the most resistant of the lot."

"And he still is. Duffer is upset that Miller's costs appear to be continuing to drop, making the potential advantage of the Hyperion Project marginal at best. In fact, those were the words Toller used with Duffer in the meeting. If that doesn't fly, I strongly suspect that Duffer will leave because he just refuses to accept the competitive advantage potential that we now seem to be on the verge of recapturing."

"Sounds like you have everything under control, Baron. But I have to admit I was worried about the outcome. There was a good chance it wouldn't have worked out this way. I guess we owe Miller for coming around. He really became the key that unlocked the door."

"I was worried, too, but if there is anyone I need to thank it's you, Warren. You were the catalyst."

"I'm glad it worked out so well."

"Better yet," Baron added. "We're already working on a revision to our corporate mission and value statements. We are putting the triple bottom line of economics, equity and environment at the core of everything we do."

The environment opens up
many opportunities for people.
Self interest will help drive their action.
Therefore, show them the light.

So What?…Environmental concerns
are everyone's.

Be an ***ecolutionist*** leader
and seize the opportunity.

EPILOGUE

We hope that The Green Baron has been inspirational for you and challenge you to look for applications in your own firm. Remember, action without thought is liable to take you where you don't want to go, and thought without action will get you nowhere fast. If anything registers from this reading, let it be this: critical thought plus a willingness to engage will enable you to do great things.

Need something else to challenge you? How about your facilities? How about the lights? The insulation? The power sources and usage? The windows? Putting the power of green to your buildings will lead you to another wheelbarrow full of savings and position your firm to take advantage of the triple bottom line. Lead by example in your world.

Our challenge to you: be the *ECOLUTION!!!!!!!!!*

ISBN 142511164-5

9 781425 111649